The Curve of Forgotten Things

D1422296

The Curve of Forgotten Things

Mark Geffriaud

Book Works, 2012

1 / THE CURVE OF FORGOTTEN THINGS

Things slowly curve out of sight

until they are gone. Afterwards

   only the curve

   remains.

—Richard Brautigan

Preface

I heard that an Argentinean writer would have declared one day that it is madness to write books. That it is better to pretend those books already exist and to simply provide a summary or a commentary. I recently had one of those books in my hands. I'm just finishing it at this time. The ideas written down are the type that are read or written but which, outside the words that pin them down, don't remain in place. And the only way to retain some traces or images will have been to launch myself immediately into writing its preface. I won't depart from the rules that have determined the genre and which aim to introduce the reader not so much to the book itself as to the moment when he will have finished reading it and when the image that he will have formed of its totality will equally have begun to dissipate. In short, these lines will introduce only the narration of a blink of an eye. **Haggard, he'd finally raised his head.**
The time for an idea, a thought, an image to appear and get the hell out. How much time then to catch up with it? That depends on the hunter, of course. But even more on his ingenuity to lose himself rather than on his skill at tracking it down. As the old adage says, in order to find something

that you think is lost, you'd better start by losing yourself.

Useless then to turn around. Not that the method is bad as such, it would be rather good in fact, providing one knew how to do a U-turn correctly. A half-degree more or a half-degree less and the whole caboodle drifts away. You could then spend all your life rectifying the trajectory in order to come back if only to yesterday's toast. That is why, beyond the keys found at the cost of an exhausting backward walk in the few square metres of your flat, the pursuit of such an approach in the suburbs of your memory will prove too often to be draining and lead only to a quick dive into an obscure perplexity.

As always, the return distance would not depend on the outward distance. Or, to put it differently, there wasn't any outward distance. So it wouldn't seem really necessary to rush, even if you'd put the ardour of that pilot, who in 1965, after falling at a speed approaching 1,000 kilometres per hour instantly threw himself into a race of another type, by narrating for one hour thirty-five minutes the story of the eight point seven seconds his loss of control had lasted.

His eyes had remained locked a few dozen centimetres from his face. The visual fog around him formed a single continuous obstacle on which his eyes came to softly bounce before going back in the other direction. It seemed to him he was looking behind his eyes, and

distinguishing deep in them the slow undulations of his ulterior motives.

For all that, I wouldn't want to make the apology of a restless wandering, no more than of an alcoholic perception entirely absorbed by the saga of a moment. The reason is I am not trying to make the apology for anything, but simply to find again the feeling of thrill and confusion that will have accompanied the disappearance of an emerging idea. An idea that will have fed on the progressive dissipation of the terms of its enunciation and will, because of that, have had no duration whatsoever.

> **A shape had intrigued him, and he had let himself be guided by that bait, trying to catch its outlines. Led deeper still, he had ended up piercing the fog and taking bearings on the trace of tape just opposite, on the window.**
> **Thinking he was sinking, he had resurfaced.**

You are going nowhere, even to your downfall, without some idea in your head. I heard that one day and I've retained it ever since. Without any old pole star, it's true, even getting lost becomes a headache. Thus I will have made myself a compass with an extract of a Buddhist text that will have crossed 8,000 kilometres and 2,000 years to tell us that 'the world is shattered and resuscitated six thousand five hundred million times a day and every man is an illusion,

vertiginously constructed by a
series of instantaneous and
solitary men.'
That vision, rather dispiriting at
first – *in the end, I will not even have met
myself* – will also have dissipated
the threat of repetition by
guaranteeing everything and
everyone a constant renewal – *I
will always have just arrived*. No
beginning, nor end, it will always
have been the first and only time.
A bit like when you catch yourself
in the middle of an action whose
finality has eluded you on the
way. What have I come to get
here? A pen? A lighter? A book?
The truth? A jumper? I don't think
so, I'm not cold. My posture could
have shown me I was in the
process of bending down. To open
a drawer? To pick up something
from the floor? Or to gather
momentum before jumping onto
the chair? But from there, what?
Too late, the position of my legs,
my arms, the bow of my head, the
spread of my fingers, all will
quickly have collapsed in a
disorder of short-lived
hypotheses.

> **Even before being conscious of it,
> his gaze had passed through the
> window, bumping against a tree
> trunk, skidding on the leaves,
> onto the building behind, to hit
> the water tower in the distance
> and shatter amongst the
> buildings right at the back. The
> landscape appeared to him in all
> its familiar singularity.**

By tripping over, you sometimes
distance yourself slightly from
the smooth unfolding of events.
Who knows if, by lingering a bit

longer, you wouldn't succeed in
getting rid of a cumbersome
future, and enjoying the sight of
an entirely clear horizon. That is
probably why, if it's true that the
world will always belong to those
who get up early, the latecomers
will nevertheless enjoy the secret
privilege of leaving it to them
willingly.
Being late is not being where
you should be. That's understood.
But if you look at it from the other
side, you'll see that you're also
where you're not expected.
Ambiguous pleasure that is paid,
it's true, at the price of a quasi-
unanimous disapprobation.
I should be there and I am here.
I've got nothing to do here.
So I have all the time in the
world.

The view was rather clear and
formed a coherent arrangement
of foregrounds and backgrounds
whose outline was even more
accentuated by the oblique light.
While he had lingered on the
most vivid fringe on the horizon,
the darkness around him had
become more pressing. As if
aware of a threat, his attention
had slightly swerved to the right,
accomplishing a backward jump
of some dozen kilometres before
initiating a slide on the wall, the
angle of the wall, the plant the
shelf the table the armchair the
floor the skirting board the wall,
the image pinned on the wall, the
image he had seen a million
times perhaps, that he hadn't
looked at since he had hung it
there, facing his desk, and that
however stirred his curiosity now

that the penumbra had partially subtracted it from his gaze.

The latecomers will have irritated more than one with their bad sportsmanship. Always looking for excuses, negotiating the rules of the game, or plainly ignoring them. But one shouldn't confuse bad sport with bad loser, or with bad faith. A real bad sport, a let's say sincere bad sport, experiences the incompatibility between two versions of reality, his own and, more often, that of the referee. That rather depressing postulate – *I see things better than everybody else, I cannot be mistaken* – will have reached at times a true tragicomic dimension – *your decision negates my existence, the world is not big enough for the two of us*. Let's just remember the stunning stupefaction of John McEnroe before his fits of anger, to realise that he was not so much trying to take the point away from his opponent than he was struggling with all his rage to escape from the referee's mind. And what he kept on screaming at him, year after year, hoping to wake him up one day, is that he flatly refused for his game to be ruled by the hallucination of some small high-perched accountant. The conflict in the end will have perhaps aimed not so much at deciding between two versions of a fact as at determining who its author really was.

He had made a move to turn the light on and shed light on the image in front of him but fortunately had changed his mind to avoid making the night fall too suddenly.

Children seem to understand that better than anyone else and even organised it into a game, known in France as *un deux trois soleil*. The game confronts two visions, that of the players and that of the leader who also acts as a referee. The players must reach the wall without being seen moving while the referee tries to catch them in motion. The players pretend they haven't moved, the referee's looking for proof to the contrary. The game invariably ends the same way. The leader can punish some players by sending them back to the starting line, that way only delaying the moment of his own defeat, without however being able to avoid it. One of the players will inevitably end up appearing suddenly at his back, hitting the wall and screaming 'sun' before him. They will then swap places and roles and the game will start again. The only finality will have been in the swapping itself. Neither gain nor real victory, the winner of the game is already about to lose the next one.

The whole game will have thus generated the constant circulation on which it feeds.

One two three

Before one of the players manages to touch the wall, the leader will

His hand instead had closed on his watch, the feeling of just arriving making him think it was high time to leave.
It would have been enough for him to get up,

to gather his spirit,

to gather his things,

to slip into his coat,

one arm,

then another,

and to go through the door.

Then he would still have had to press the switch.
To turn the light on in the corridor.
To quickly sweep the darkness with his gaze.
And to close the door.

To look for the keyhole.

have regularly turned around to
beat time and give a tempo to the
race happening behind his back,
multiplying the syncopations to
try to deceive his players.

To find the keyhole.

Doing that he will also have
orchestrated his own fall.

**To introduce the key into the
keyhole.**
To turn the key in the keyhole.

All against the referee, that's the
key. The excitement of the players
will have fed on the contradictory
feeling of wanting to come ever
closer to the one from whom they
will have tried to avoid all along,

Once.
Twice.

runaways throwing themselves
into some kind of backwards
escape.

**Not to linger on the details
of the door.
The colour of the door.
The yellow light of the bulb
bouncing against the paint on
the door,
against the metal of the keyhole.
To take the key out of the
keyhole,
the door ten centimetres from his
eyes,**

Sun!

**the door stretching as far as the
eye can see.**

Each time the leader suddenly
turns around, he will have
interrupted the action. In the
blink of an eye the players will
have petrified in a single forward
move, suspended in their shared
will to not be noticed.
I saw you moving!

No, I did not!
To turn away from the door.

Bad faith and self-persuasion will
have been the key elements in
that well-oiled scenario.

To turn around in the corridor.

Action!
As soon as the chosen player
has taken his initial position
again,

To turn around towards the
stairs.

The banister.
The banister stretching from the
top to the bottom of the stairs.

the leader will have resumed
counting up to three while
pounding the wall in front of
him,

From the skylight to the
dustbins,

turning his back on the action,

from the skylight to the smell of
the dustbins.

hearing only the sound,
the sound of his own voice,
the sound of his own pounding,

To the echo of the entrance hall.
At the front door to the building.
At the creaking of the front door.
At the weight of the door.
At the sharp banging of the door.

the sound of a group of children
charging at him as one,
snapping at his heels,
ready to take cover at the slightest
risk of being discovered,
but also ready to pounce at the
first opportunity.

At the detonation in his back.
Amplified by the hall.

By the echo in the hall.

Like a shot in the night.
Fired anywhere
anyhow.
Without aiming.
Just like that, for fun.
Just like that, at random.
Because the shot has been fired.
And you hadn't had the time to
think about it.

Cut!

For there had been all the time in
the world to think about it after.

Hey you,

All the time in the world to strain
your ears.

what the fuck are you doing here!

go back there!

A strange scene in which
directing the actors will have been
given to the victim. However, at
no time will he have been able to
intervene in the script. And if the
ending will have been known in
advance,

To wait for the impact.
To follow the trajectory of the
bullet into his head.
Searching for an obstacle to
penetrate
an obstacle on which to bounce
back
on which to crash
somewhere to go
to go and crash
become compact
gather oneself like the building
had gathered itself behind him
slightly more shrunken at each
step
disappearing with the distance
like a child's drawing traced with
a finger on his back
like an architectural plan faded
crumpled and thrown in a ball in
the corner of his mind
shrivelling up at the sound of the
gravel under his shoes

at the sound of gravel in the
night
alternating with the friction of
his trousers
the friction of the air against his
ears
the friction of a bullet shot
anywhere anyhow in the night.
Why?
Just have to wait to know.
Straining your ear.
Waiting for the answer to arrive
by itself from over there.
From where?
unsurprisingly he will have seen   Waiting for the echo.
nothing coming.

Maybe because the story, had
differed the expected and dreaded
event for so long that it had
simply been left behind. Hard to
say at that point if it will have
been wiser to wait for it or   To walk in the direction of the
                                       echo to make it arrive sooner
                                       to hear sooner what had just
                                       happened
                                       what had just happened
                                       elsewhere.
                                       To arrive elsewhere sooner
                                       where something or someone
                                       had been waiting for you.
                                       An impact.
                                       A fixation.
                                       A delay.
                                       A delay of one hundredth.
                                       A delay of a thousandth on
                                       yourself.
                                       Like the sound running after the
                                       image.
                                       Like the sound with the image.
                                       To arrive before the image
to flee.

                                       and set up an ambush for it.
                                       Set a trap for yourself.
                                       To station somewhere.

To wait on the verge.
At the side of a summer road,
on a straight expanse of hot
tarmac
a straight line as far as the eye
can see
still and inflexible
unless you drive at high speed
and don't take your eyes off the
road
and tear along
driving towards the light
against the light
against all that useless light
that light with no obstacle
no obstacle from the sun to the
windscreen
shattering into pieces
shattering into pieces against the
glassy surface of your eyes
forcing its way through the
pinhole
of your half-closed eyes
weary from all that useless light
all that light with no obstacle
all that warmth with no image
that had landed on his retina
all those images that had etched
their absence
a purple absence
an elusive absence
a second of absence
barely a second
a fraction of a second
a hundredth of an absence
just the time to jump at the
opportunity
the time to refresh your ideas
the time to jump in the river
to get a bit cooler

I remember having read in a study
devoted to allegorical cartography
that an anonymous essay would
have initiated a kind of
topography of thought. This

attempt would present itself as a
list still waiting to be followed up
after almost a hundred years'
interruption. I will often have
wondered what it would end up
looking like if each generation
contributed to it. I would propose
the thought that you are on the
verge of becoming but do not
know anything about yet

the thought that always presents
itself in a new light

the thought that presents itself in
profile

the thought you immediately
replace with another

the thought you would have
preferred never to have

to have a dip in the frozen river
the river forcing its way through
the shady forest
a quick dip into its dark waters
a quick dip into the mirror of a
moonless night
just a little dip before making a
campfire
before gathering some wood in
the dark forest
grilling some fish
caught in the river
in the icy river that had caught
you unaware that very morning
and left you shivering under a
rare sun
a sun barely filtering through the
mist
barely filtering through the
numerous tiers of leaves
superimposing the shadows from
above with the shadows from
below

before falling to the ground in
fine dust
a sun barely filtering through the
mist
before bouncing back on the
muddy waters of the river
the opaque waters that had
firmed up your muscles
and firmed up your mind
that had put you back on your
feet
put you back on the lookout.
On the lookout for what?
On the lookout for the slightest
movement

the slightest movement in the
leaves
the slightest apparition in the
firing line of your rifle
ready to welcome the unexpected
the perspective of the

the thought you wonder why you
hadn't had earlier

unexpected in the thickness of
the forest
a vanishing point
a landmark if you want
the assurance to walk straight
ahead

the thought that fades for being
contemplated

with an idea in mind and a focal
point on the horizon.
To bring the idea closer to the
point, that's the idea.

the thought you are neither ready
to welcome nor capable of chasing
away

The fixed idea.

the thought that takes on
frightening proportions at night
but hides in the morning among
your socks
the thought you try to place at any
given opportunity

The repeated idea.

the thought you don't have the
heart to push back but that goes
against your convictions
the thought you don't want either
to share or to keep for yourself
the thought that comes out of
who knows what and leads who
knows where

One foot after the other, in
rhythm.

the thought that always remains
enigmatic and that you welcome
each time as a childhood friend

Without thinking about it.
Nothing but the idea and the
point.
The point that had grown.
That had taken shape.
That had resembled less and less
the idea.

That had made the idea change.
The point that had not been a point.
The point that had been a shape.
A shape that had moved.
Barely.
But nevertheless.
A shape that had moved forward.
Moved straight ahead.
A shape similar to yours.
With an idea in mind.
With what idea in mind?
A shape that had thought.
Thought what?
Thought about the shape in front of it.
Thought about the idea you had in mind.
What idea in mind?
An idea that had changed.
An idea that had talked.
A voice that had thought.
That had changed idea to change shape.
That had changed shape to change the idea in its mind.

the thought that makes you doubt
its existence
the thought that

And change its shape.

this list could stretch on and on.
You would only need to look for
what distinguishes each thought
from all the others rather than
repeatedly finding resemblances.
By devoting all one's time and
energy to it, one would perhaps
end up in the course of a life
approximately describing the
outlines of one single idea by
following the trajectory of its
endless metamorphoses.
Indigenous Australians would
probably welcome this remark
with a shrug, for they don't own a

A shape that had stood out more
and more clearly.

A shape less and less similar to
yours.

A shape that had taken form.

territory but only its crossing.
Anyway that's what a friend of
mine told me who heard it from
one of his, who I think had read it
somewhere and to who, in
exchange, I will have told how the
Achuars, a Jivaro tribe, had the
custom of starting each of their
encounters with a ceremonial
conversation during which host
and visitor looked straight into
each other's eyes while talking at
the same time.
No precedence of the question
over the answer, all will have
happened at the same time.
I will often have described that
ritual to friends, renewing each
time my enthusiasm as when
reading the first lines of a novel
that promises to be thrilling but
whose following pages would be
missing. However, years would
pass before I re-read the few lines
that describe it in the last quarter
of a book on misunderstanding,
before I refer to the note at the
bottom of the page and discover
the name of the author quoted,
Maurizio Gnerre,

before I obtain his article that was
accompanied by

a recording he had made of that
ritual a few years before my birth,

of two voices superimposed on a
magnetic tape,

before I write to him and finally
go to visit him

in Rome.

That you had no longer taken

your eyes off.

That hadn't let you out of its

sight.

Already within earshot.

A stranger's face,

as a whole.

But familiar,

in the details.

A nose.

Lips.

Ears.

Eyebrows.

Already seen all that somewhere.

Assembled differently.

Fix a precise point on his face.

To hold it all in place.

A landmark.

In the unknown.

A fellow creature.

A brother.

My Brother Did You Come?

Conversation between anthropological linguist Maurizio Gnerre and Mark Geffriaud,
Rome, 2011

Does it always start like that, with
that same sentence,
my brother did you come?

> Usually yes.
> *Yatsúru winyámek,*
> yes.

It's rather an uncommon question
when you are face to face with
someone.

> There is a performative aspect
> here
> which is not being surprised.
> You are an important person,
> you are the chief of this
> household,
> you are there
> and the attitude is like saying
> Ok, did you come?
> I mean the attitude is not to say
> Oh! Are you here?
> It's not that.
> You have a deep and very wide
> vision of the world
> sort of ok,
> I was waiting for you,

I knew you were coming.

> you are here now.
> And you show that you are
> absolutely quiet
> you have no reasons to be either
> excited or worried.
> You are very self-confident,
> you're in your household
> and of course the person who is
> coming
> has to announce himself
> Pouuuu!
> before he comes
> so he shows that he's coming as
> a friend,

hum

not as an enemy.
And so even if you don't know
this guy
because maybe he comes from a
remote place,
maybe you've seen him only once
in your life
but twenty years ago when he
was a child
or whatever...
So you say this sentence
Yatsúru winyámek
which means my brother are you
here,
did you come,

hum

ok, sit down,

yes

showing that you are absolutely
not worried
about anything.

and what happens next?

Then you start to actually ask
why did you come?
Or depending,
who are you?
Usually a person who comes to
pay a visit
knows the other in one sense or
another,
or if they don't know each other
at least they have some relation,
I am the son of such and such,
at least that.
Then starts this ritual
communication
during which they speak in a very
special way
almost a coded way of
communication,
very fast and with all these
peaks,
a sort of ritualised way,
we could even use the term
poetic,
because you have to put things
together

using key words, fiting them in
ritual patterns.
And this is a way of presenting
yourself.
And the other one,
let's say the chief of the
household or the main person
asks you
why this and that
and then you exchange.

Actually what is quite surprising
when you read the transcription
is that they use almost the same
sentences   yes
or the same blocks   yes yes
as if everything that was said   yes
belonged to both.
So if you don't see the
conversation,
how would you tell who is who?
Who is the host and who the
visitor?

It is possible to recognise that.
For instance the chief of the
household,
the one who is being visited
uses a verb which is very
important in their ideology,
pujajai!
hum hum   which means I stay, I exist, I stay,
meaning I am the person of this
house,
I'm here.
Whereas the person who is
visiting says things like *winyajai!*
or *listin!*
to visit I came,
so it's clear who is who.

Ah it's that clear?

Absolutely clear.
Although you're right,
there is an important specularity
and symmetry that could reflect
an ideology of relatively equal
relations.

They also stare at each other and
speak at the same time,
almost like a mirror that would
send back a different image
than the one it received.

If you are a grown-up man,
who's really secure towards how
to behave,
you can watch the other one in
the eyes.
If you are not so secure
or if you feel sort of
uncomfortable,
you'd better watch like that.

And is there a big difference if you
are looking or not?

hum

You don't feel so brave,
you don't feel so secure of your
position
and of your knowledge of the
way to behave.

hum

In a world where there is all this
etiquette
regarding behaviour and speech
and so on,
it's not only about knowing the
language,
it's knowing much more
and sometimes youngsters are
sent by their parents to pay a
visit and they're really scared
because they could do a terrible
performance,
lose the rhythm of the speech or
say silly things,
I'm here but I don't know why or
whatever
and women can even laugh and
so...

Yes hum...
So it is a kind of territory.

Yes

Let's say a symbolic territory

Hum hum... hum hum

that not anybody can enter

Hum hum

and hum... this territory only
appears if you can perform the
dialogue

Hum hum

enter in the right way

**Ritual communication is a
setting.
You perform your own drama in
your own setting.
So it's a sort of frame,
Goffman's idea of a frame of
action.
So it's not so obvious that
anybody could come and say hey
I also come to talk here.**

Yes **No, there's a frame.**
And is it the same frame that they
enter
from one ceremonial dialogue to
another?

Hum hum... yeah

The same space that appears each
time?

**You should see who the actors
are.**

Yeah...

**Even if they don't really know
each other,
they perform as if they do.
The idea is always I know you,
I know who you are and I was
waiting for you.**

Hum hum

Yatsúru winyámek,
that's the idea

So it's a matter of identity and
distance,
as if they travelled the last metres
between them
on a metaphorical or symbolic
level or something no?

Hum hum

And is there a relation between

this distance,
I mean spatial and social distance
and the length of the
conversation?
The further the longer?

Basically so.
At that time, they basically didn't
have any neighbours,
there were these big long houses
in the forest
and there was nothing around,
I mean you had to walk two or
three hours
to reach another one.
So there were no villages and this
is very important.
Social distance was related to an
idea,
sort of a mental map of kinship.
Who are you in terms of
relations?
And also, edging a dangerous
situation,
you could also be part of a group
that was
or even still is an enemy of mine.

Yes

So here we are even edging a
very dangerous situation.
Sometimes this could end up by
saying
ok let's go to sleep
and in the night killing the guy
who was visiting
or the opposite
the visitor killing the main person
of the house
and so on.
So there are all these issues of
negotiating distance.
And the length of the dialogue,
of the performance,
is related to how much distance
or even possible social and
political attrition
should be solved or released.

So it is sort of a medicine
for social and political tension.

hum
but if somebody comes to kill you
that way,

but they don't do it that directly

no

while they're sitting and talking
no, never, no,
that's impossible

so they would first go through the
ceremonial dialogue

the etiquette is very important

yes

so first you talk and discuss and

you wouldn't come out of the
forest

no

and kill someone

no,
you talk and you drink
and you go to sleep
and maybe during the night you
kill the person
or you wait for him to walk out
to release some water on the
ground
and while that
puff!!!

ok so

Pah!!!

the ceremonial conversation is
also a way of checking

Yes, it's a way of checking,
it's a first way of checking.
Let's say something of a first
filter

yes

to understand why you are here,
who you are
and after that you can decide
ok this is a good guy, no problem
or I know everybody in his family
and so on,
they are not enemies of mine.

yes...

and so some of the time,
not all the time,
but some of the time
they speak at the same time
on top of each other

    yes yes
    at the same time, at the same
    time

like that

    yes yes yes yes yes

and so when you do that
you cannot listen to what the
other person is saying

    exactly exactly

so at that point who is that
conversation for?
I mean,
do you think the conversation has
its own life in a way?

    It's the performance for the
    performance.
    What ethnomusicologists call
    heterophony.
    You don't need to be silent and
    listen
    to the one who's saying or
    singing,
    you do it at the same time.
    So the idea is that the
    performance
    has its own value in itself.

yes
    Performance should go ahead
yeah yeah
    no matter if someone is listening
    to what I'm saying
hum
    or understanding what I'm
    saying.

so it's no more about meaning

    at some point meaning is
    absolutely blurred,
    erased
    and performance in itself is
    what's important

yes

    and...
hum hum
    for instance in China there are
    these poems
    on stone ground, travertine, a
    very porous stone,

yes
yeah yeah

hum

it receives the water.
So, they have water here,
and they do like that,
there is a poem to be written
in ideograms.
Here...
that's it.
It's only water.
I've seen this done let's say at
2pm in Shanghai,

yeah
it disappears
hum hum

the sun is really hot.
In a few moments it's erased
so the value is the performance
in itself
it's not for people to say oh ah
how beautiful and so on

no

there is a performance
and it is completely erased in a
short time

yes

and that's it.
Nobody has to say oh great.

so at that point what is important
is the music or let's say
the expression and the apparition
of the space between them,
I mean,
if they're speaking at the same
time and not listening,
it's not what it means any more
but what it does that

Yeah the important thing is that
you talk,
you speak and that's it,
why should you know exactly
what I am saying?
Whereas the transcriber,
let's say me when I was doing
that,
you want to understand exactly
what they were saying.
And so it's a long work and very
painful
and you reach some transcription
but in a sense,
from a local point of view, it's

irrelevant I mean,
they're just performing.
It's our way of understanding the
world
that is providing meaning to
everything
that we want to provide meaning
to
but in that sense the only
relevant meaning
is the one he has in his brain
and that's for himself and not for
somebody else,

hum...

when they speak together like
this

22   warí túmashtainkyá
     what it is done this way

     warí ántsar kétkurish áusha
     what this way we stay at home
     ya
     who

23   warí ántsar pujákrisha
     what this way staying

     warí jiniskeka kémtainkyá
     what without visiting staying

24   jiímkachuka kémtainkya
     without visiting staying at
     home

     warí tímyaju tsúru
     what that much my

     áusha ya
     brother who

25   warí kémtaka kémtainkya
     what staying staying

     yá kémtaka áusha
     who staying

26   warí tú tútukimtsuk wekátash
     what so so saying this you go
     wekamtaiya
     going

     warí tímyajuka
     what that much staying
     kémtainkya
     at home

27

     tú tútukimtsuk áusha yá
     so so saying   who

27a ja jai

28

     wekátanash wekájaiya
     going   I go

28a maa

29

     warí tímyaju tsúru aushá
     what that much my brother

29a jm

30

     nuíkya nuíkya tsúru aushá
     before before my brother

30   jai

31

     júnik pujákminkya
     without anything if you stay
     tsúru aushá
     my brother

31a ja warí tumashtainkyá
     what it is done this way

32 káme ántsarik kétkursha
    this way staying at home

                                   ya wayásan tsúru aushá
                                   who I am entering the
                                   house my brother

    jiímtsuka keemtá
    without visiting you have to stay

33 irásmin ayátkun tútunish
    visiting begin able around
    wekékini
    there going

                                     warí jínyantá wísha
                                   what without seeing I
                                   kináchkun
                                   also am leaving

34 wayása jiímkyachu
    entering the house without
    ekét wéajai
    visiting the house staying I go

                                       já wéakun jiímtsuk
                                   sick I am going without
                                   pujú wéajai
                                   visiting staying I go

35 ja warí ántsar kétkursha
    sick what this way staying

                                       warí warí tímya áusha yá
                                   what what said   who

36 jiímkyachu kémtainkya
    without visiting staying

                                       warí tímya tsúru áusha yá
                                   what said my brother who

37 yatsúta tímyaujainkiá
    between brothers with such

                                       warí trúakun tsúru áusha yá
                                   what I am doing so my
                                   brother who

    inyáischamuka awítya
    without seeing it should not be
    (how is it possible for brothers
    to live without visiting?)

38 warí ekéttutikyá aushá
    what I stay in my house

                                       ekéttutikya áusha tá
                                   I stay in my house

39 wajaté wajaté wajaténkyaityá
    stop and wait stop and wait

                                       warí ekéttutikya aushá
                                   what I stay in my house

40 warí túra wekátsumeash
    what so doing you come to visit

                                       warí imyá
                                   what that
                                   (u)ntsuríchuka aushá
                                   much many

41   warí tímyajush áawitya
                                   what that much has to see

41a jm jm

42   tú tútukin yatsúru
so saying this my
tímyaju aushá
brother that much

42a jm
43   yá yamáya juí se aushá
who now here

43a jai
44   twí twí tukí áusha yá
where where I am saying

44a jm
45   ya aé akunchá
who this way
áusha ya
although he stays

45a chua
46   ma aé akunchá áusha
this way although he stays

46a jentá
47   wainyásan jínanta (u)kúakun
entering seeing leaving
(going back without seeing)

47a jentá
48   yá túrusan tímyaju satá
who the same like
this you stay

48a jm jm
49   wi túnantaku tsúru aushá
I saying this way my brother

49a jae
50   yá tsúmash ukumajá
who saying I left

50a jentá
51   tú tútnyaku tsurú áusha yá
so saying my brother who

51a jm

so, so when they speak together
like that,
is it very different from one
ceremonial dialogue
to another?

As long as I know,
not so much
because I think at that point,
when they get to the point of
speaking together,
several things they've already
said come back.

hum   **So they repeat.**
So in a sense, it's a way of playing
with the fact that I've already
said something.
Now I repeat that,
so if they speak together that's
fine, I mean...
in a sense what had to be said
has been said.

Ah, so when they cross their
voices,
they are repeating, going back.
So as they're negotiating a   **yeah of course of course**
distance,
is it also the moment
when they finally get to the same   **yes yes absolutely**
point,
as if the distance had been
                                       it's
covered?
                                       hum hum
So they're speaking the same
moment
and the same space
but in two different ways   **yeah**
coming back together at the same   **yeah**
time
to what has already been said   **yes**
from two different directions
crossing their trajectories as if
the point was   **at this point**
                                       graphically or visually
                                       I could represent it as going like

that
like that
like that

yes

at this point you come back
and it starts again
differently

yes

it's like a dance

like a dance yeah

yes

because also before the
ceremonial
there is total silence no?
more or less

... yes ...
that's very important ...

but during the ceremonial
there are no breaks

no no never breaks

never silence

no no no no no
There is silence before they start.
And silence after they end.

hum hum

So the guy comes there,
the visitor,
he sits down,
usually with his spear here or,
these days he comes with his
gun,
sits there.
The head of the household,
the main person,
very slowly starts painting his
face,
putting his hair in a nice way,
if he has a crown, puts the crown
on and all that,
very slowly,
showing that he is absolutely
easy, no problem
and so on.
So there is all this moment of
silence
and nothing happens at that

point,
only him preparing himself
and so on.
At some point he says
Yatsúru winyámek,
my friend did you come?
And then starts the dialogue.
When they finish, they finish in
an amazing way,
just — clack! — together

how ...?
how does it ...?

silence

At that point, they finish
together,
usually the chief of the house
says something,
aha, which means ok
and this is the signal saying stop,
ok.
And after that, some minutes of
absolute silence follow.
And most of the time I got the
impression that
there was some kind of tension
at this point.
Nobody was doing anything,
only children running around
while they had stopped doing
anything and so on
and after that they would start
talking
what we would call regular talk.
No question like why did you
come,
they are not going back.

So the silence
is the boundary in a way.

yes,
in a sense, yeah.
In a sense, their performance is a
sort
of parenthesis between two
silences,
before and after,
and that's it. And so

it's also a way of putting this
performance
into evidence, it's very neat. And
so
that is also an interesting idea,
I hadn't thought too much about
it before, that
while there are two voices
on top of the other in the middle,
the cuts at the beginning and at
the end
are clear and neat.

and how is the space affected by
this ceremonial dialogue?

Well
they sit at a distance that could
be,
minimum as we are now, let's say
three metres minimum
but sometimes much more.
They could sit sometimes, let's
say
from where you are to there,
so seven, eight metres distance
and the voice
is strong and everywhere in the
household
you can hear what they are
saying.
Nobody is speaking while this is
happening.
There is absolute silence around.

And this space is totally

The household is usually,
were,
now they're not any more,
households were very large,
very very big, really very big,
with these immense roofs and
the part for men
and the part for women
and of course the dialogue was
performed
in the part for men and
it was very very large, very large

and
sometimes they were sitting all
around
and even if the visitors were two
or three men
or even more sometimes and in
the house
there was a chief, a main person,
and two other second and third
men
in the scale of the hierarchy of
the household,
ceremonial conversation was
always
only one to one,
one to one, one to one.
In their conception of speech,
they never had the idea of, till
very recent times,
of one speaking to many.
There is this story
from the end of the nineteenth
century,
there is a tale, well not a tale,
an account that took place in
1891,
one very early traveller went
there and so on
and he tells the story of one of
them
who travelled far away,
up to the Amazonian town,
Amazonian Peruvian town of
Iquitos
and he was there and he saw for
the first time
a square where, I don't know, the
army,
a general or whatever

hum

was talking to the troops
and he was absolutely struck to
see that one man

ahaha

could speak at the same time to
so many

yes

which was absolutely new

because the idea was always one
to one,
face to face conversation,
not one to many. And so
he came back and became a very
important warrior.
He was called Nanki Jukima,
which actually is an interesting
name
because the literal translation
into English
would be Shakespeare,

ahaha

Shake-Spear

yes

Nanki Jukima is this action

ahahaha

to shake a spear.
And this *Nanki Jukima* had the idea
that he could put together many
many men,
warriors I mean important
people, big guys
and talk to all of them
and they couldn't believe that
one was speaking to many.

Hum...

Because the idea is that speech
should be exerted only one to
one.

So many people can listen...

of course, listen

but you can't talk to...

exactly.

And so when there are several
people visiting

yeah

does it happen that several
ceremonial conversations

yes yes

can it start, can all of it
mix or not

can start, can start

this is exactly
in line with the idea of
heterophony

yes

When they have several visits
and several people
they can talk one to the other

hum

but not caring at all about what

the others are saying
even if the sound of the speech is
loud,
very loud voice and so on,
could even cover the speech of
the others,
this is exactly the idea of
heterophony.

so it can happen let's say that six
people
are talking at the same time

Six yes, two two and two

yes

three conversations

yes three conversations

they're here, two of them, one is
sitting here
and the other one is there,
and another is there...
that could happen,
and this is the maximum I've
seen

hum hum it's a bit like free jazz in
a sense

yes exactly exactly.

So here in this book which came
out some years ago
heterophony: *see under* texture
texture: performance,
heterophony.

I like this texture idea.

which is a metaphor of course

a metaphor yes

but of course
a lot of metaphors we have to
take advantage from, yes.
Texture in this big book
they say *see also* performance,
practice, register,

yeah

heterophony of course.
For instance here is an
interesting concept,
texture as a simultaneous
multiplicity of individual

ah

hum hum
what is also interesting here
is that the scene stays empty
the space between them
where the voices mix
and no one steps inside
during the performance
everybody's around but it stays
empty and

yes, and only words are thrown
inside,
well thrown,
only words can enter this scene,
something immaterial

but it seems that what appears
there
is visible for everybody...
I mean they're always talking
about home and house

and it's not very clear whose
house it is actually.
Is it this metaphorical house?
The house that is left behind? or
the house that they are
entering?
The house they are entering

because they also say things like
without visiting staying at home

hum hum

performances
simultaneous multiplicity of
individual performances

yeah
yes yes
no
no no no

and they are very quiet while
sitting.

yes

yeah yeah

no
the house they are entering

yes
but
but
yes.
But in terms of cultural ideology
that is a negative idea, the
negative idea of a man who
always stays home
and never visits, that's negative
so when they say
without visiting I always stay at
my place,
this refers to a man who is sort of

say a poor guy
with no political connection.
They also have this rhetorical
question,
should we perhaps stay at home

hum
without visiting?
Hen hen!
So there are two things here,
the big man, the important
person
who stays at home and he's
there,
Pujàhé!,
I'm here, I stay here,
but he should at least receive
plenty of visits or
go sometimes to visit people of
the same level,
and the other idea
should I always stay at home
without visiting?
That would be kind of a poor guy
who has no connection with the
others,
no alliances to make for war,
no exchange or whatever
so it's a guy who is out of the
network connections.
So it's all about who is visiting
who,

yes.
at which level and
And through all this idea of
with what frequency.
staying or leaving
their own house,
yes
there is also the negotiation of
this symbolic place,
where they are meeting

yes yes

probably meaning that's also how
it's made,
staying, leaving, coming back
in speech

I'm just thinking about
something now,

ah

45

how the households were
scattered in the forest
and so on.
Some of them could be places
through which a path
through the jungle would pass.
In that case, these are likely to
receive more visits.
But others were sort of terminals
so beyond there where do you
want to go?
So who is coming here and why?
Is he only passing by
and maybe wants to sleep here
and go ahead?
or is he coming to pay a visit?
All these are sort of subtle
political
and power dimensions of course.
So when you are visiting this
particular house,
it's a way of relating it to the
whole map.
Because they have a clear idea of
the map
of who is who and where.
I mean all these households
sometimes could be at two
hours,
three hours, five hours,
twelve hours walk one from
another,
so it's clear if you ask where you
are coming from
and where you are going
it's clear if you are just passing by
or if you actually came here.
So by knowing who is who,
where each one lives and also
asking
where you are coming from
you understand if one wants to
tell you a lie
or has some bad intention of
killing somebody

hum

yes

or whatever...
why do you come to this place?

So it's a bit like on a board game,
how and where you move
gives clues of how you see the
whole set,
how you see the relations between
the pieces
at that point

yes

and these movements also draw
the boundaries
in which they are included,
the frame of the board game.

certainly there is a very strong
idea of borders,
who's the territory of whom,
why are you here in a sense,
why did you come all the way up
to here?
You are twelve hours' walk
even more from your place,
why are you here, what is the
purpose?
You can't tell me
that you were just coming
around hunting let's say
so you are coming here for some
specific reason so,
also the level of explanation
excuses why you are here.
Controlling territories is related
to distances
and they have of course
quite a clear mental map of
distances. Of course.

And is there a ceremonial to leave?

Oh of course!
when you leave you have another
conversation
that is not usually so long and so
specific
in its shape and so on
but still when you leave there is a
way of saying

well now I leave, now I'm going,
the other one says walk well and
and... they usually don't say so
much
come back again
but something like I'll see you
some other place,
something like that
and it lasts seven to ten minutes,
it's much shorter
but there are some ritual
sentences that

Is it as codified?

yes it is

And do they also sit in a particular
place or not?

no, no

no

no,
usually, when one leaves,
the person who leaves gets up
and let's say
takes his spear and says
something like,
ok now I'm going
and the other one says,
let's say you are the main person
in the house,
ok ok yeah go go,
I'm going,
ok go go,
I will see you some other place,
so not encouraging usually
come back here to see me again,
nothing like that.
So it's something like
ok, walk well and I'll see you
some other time
some other place.

Postface

At the underground station Maurizio will have shaken my hand before retracing his steps, sheltered under his umbrella, in the streets of Rome.

As I went down the long corridor lit by a uniform light, I imagined him walking in the opposite direction in the night, and the memory of our conversation began stretching on to the superimposition of our contrary movements.

Absorbed by that thought, I rushed down the steps at high speed, any old way, lengthening or shortening my strides at the last moment, in order to catch myself unawares and see how I was going to pull through.

I reached the silent platform too quickly, badly prepared for the wait, the first of a long series. For once, I have pulled ahead too much.

Words had been exchanged,

then objects,

then words again.

Information and goods hadn't really had any value per se. The main thing had been to feed, by a constant circulation, a whole network of personal relationships. Passing from hand to hand, from head to head, words and goods hadn't generated any profit, hadn't ruined any fortune.

Nobody ever needed a map to travel the roads of bartering. Everyone had made up his own idea on the whole thing following the use he had of a portion. Stories and objects easily crossed distances that no individual had managed to cover in a lifetime and circulated freely where men didn't dare venture,

Too early to listen to the
recording.

Too excited to read.

Too late for the bottle of water.

Nothing else in my bag.
Except for the c...
Christ!
The camera!
And here I am going all the way
up the stairs again.
All the way through the corridor.
The square.
The alleyways.
Ringing the bell again.
Going up the stairs.
Mumbling excuses.
Getting the camera back.
Saying goodbye.
Going down the stairs.
Going all the way through the
alleyways the square the corridor
the stairs
only to find myself at the very
same spot,
still waiting for that damn train.

Well,
a shot for nothing
nothing more
a moment of absence, right
that just needed filling, that's all
to adjust one's aim, as they say.
Except that this time the bullet
will have ricocheted everywhere
in all directions
to the point that it will have been
impossible to grasp its course.
So even just trying to imagine it
will have been like choosing

welcome with open arms in the
deepest of hostile lands

before quietly going down the
river again

and land in the hands of a
neighbour.

By crossing and re-crossing

equally each other's territories,

they had constantly modified

their borders. Before receiving it

from a friend in exchange for

another, an object could well

have helped the cause of a

traditional enemy, and as such,

gone against one's own interests.

The bartering hadn't gone around
in a circle though, let's say it had
rather steadily moved away from
a straight line. It had acquired in
the imagination a kind of
autonomous life comparable to
that of the amoeba whose
observation had led the young
zoologist Asa Schaeffer to direct
his research to spiral movement.
He blindfolded a friend one day
and asked him to walk in a

between throwing oneself
forward or backward to take
shelter
rolled up in a ball
to take as little space as possible
eyes closed
to make oneself forgotten
while listening in my head to the
bullet hitting the ceiling lamp
radiator sink pipes
closer and closer to my head legs
arms back
as if it was the entire space that
went flying
and was gathering around a
motionless little piece of lead.
As if it was the room
that was shrivelling up on itself
like a crumpled paper,
each impact impressing a new
fold on it,
and imposing even more
promiscuity
to an ever more hostile
neighbourhood.

straight line in the middle of a
cornfield. The line of the drawing
that had followed step for step
on a piece of paper the forward
motion of his friend had
described a series of concentric
loops before crashing into a small
rectangle symbolising a tree
stump. By suddenly coming to an
end a few metres from his
departure point, his trajectory
had opened a way to posterity for
the proto-zoologist.
But if the old adage according to
which you go around in circles in
the dark when you think you are
walking straight had found its
confirmation here, it is in a
totally different experiment that
the faithful friend had also taken
part. For a brief moment, he had
in his hands two incompatible
pieces of a same fractured reality.
On one hand the cause, on the
other the consequence.

I shall have remained for another
moment with my eyes closed
after the space had finished
compacting
like a plastic wrapping around the
last chocolate.
And with it the sensation that I
was going to wake up in a new
Middle Ages
rid of the perspective
where objects

whatever the distance
would keep the dimension they
will have had in my hands.
I will first have rejoiced at the idea
of having everything now at my
disposal
before considering the various
drawbacks of a world with no
distance.
Each time I will have wanted to
move, everything will have begun
stirring with me.
In comparison taking full face in
the dark
a wall that should have been a
good three metres further off
will have seemed a rather
desirable fate
and it is therefore natural that I
will have chosen to keep my eyes
closed

I will have made a gesture to probe
the darkness all around but would
fortunately have changed my
mind to avoid making obstacles
spring up everywhere. My hands
instead will have fallen back

Usually that kind of dilemma doesn't present great difficulty. A five-years-old child knows how to have the bedroom in which the day before he has fallen asleep top-to-tail swivel around in his head. Except that here, his memory was not at issue, his legs had well and truly crossed a great distance, but a part of him had lagged behind. All his senses,

softly at my sides, the feeling of having stepped behind the scenes making me think that I didn't have much to lose anymore. I will have been able to start walking then, nonchalantly following an imaginary straight line, convinced that I would end up somehow finding my way.

A voice in my head will have helped me hold my course.

weary of being subordinated to sight had taken the opportunity of its absence to give it the slip and follow their own path. By removing the blindfold, the recollection of the walk that he had accomplished but hadn't actually happened, had most probably clung to his memory like a ghost limb. But a few seconds later the graft of his friend's narration had already taken hold. And it is undoubtedly with difficulty that he had tried later to remember the confusion that had taken hold of him when he had opened his eyes and that he had perhaps sometimes told like a story which had happened to someone else.

Hot?

Icy

Hot?

Tepid

And here?

Burning!

Over here?

Hot

And there?

Cold

I will have instinctively found the right distance from the fire. Sitting down cross-legged, the smarting of heat on my face

will already have made me forget
the cold pinching at my back.
A real splendour that campfire!
Wonderful, I swear.
Without even mentioning that
splendid fish
whose grilled skin will have taken
the colour of the best brown
really fresh
well-grilled
just out of the river
drawn on the surface along an
invisible line
drawn on the surface of the icy
river
in which I will have dived that
very morning
which will have firmed up my
muscles.
And firmed up my mind.
Which will have put me back on
my feet.
put me back on the lookout.
The lookout for what?
For danger?
A movement in the leaves
the smallest sound beyond the
wall of darkness
that the intensity of the fire will
have erected all around me
which perhaps it will have been
better for me to face
by turning my back to the fire
so as not to risk being caught
unawares
and having to turn around with a
start
turn around quickly in the forest
quickly in my bed
slightly too quickly
much too quickly
way too quickly for the curve
for the curve that the speed will
have made appear suddenly right
in the middle of the straight line

by swerving a little from the centre
of gravity
from the centre of gravity which
will have given way under the
pressure of that circular movement
which will have given way against
the partitions of the beginning of a
dream
just when I will have begun falling
asleep.
And stopped forcing my way
letting the images come naturally to
me
letting them form themselves from
behind
just before turning in my bed.
Turning in my dream.
And passing through.

Pff!!!!

Postface

Pah!!!

A certain number of games aim
at generating accident. They
differ from the games of chance
whose random aspect is the
premise by aiming at it as a
finality. One of the oldest,
invented two thousand years
ago, has spread everywhere
under the name *stone paper
scissors*.

Facing one another and swaying
their fists back to front while
shouting at the same time the
three same words, the two
players pound an invisible
obstacle with the regularity of a
stone breaker. On the third, they
both throw their hands in front of
them, forming in a blink of an eye
one of the three signs
corresponding to the three words
pronounced. Their gestures until
then perfectly synchronised,

suddenly clash. From that friction
a sparkle of disagreement
appears.
Stone
Paper
Scissors!

The view will now be suddenly
clear
everything will have fallen apart.
Nothing left behind
and nothing yet in front.

The game actually often served
the purpose of settling a dispute.

Barely a bracing sensation left by
a letter? A drawing? A poem?
on the porous surface of my
memory
a series of tangled lines
traced with a finger on my back by
a clumsy child
a series of open lines incapable of
closing on themselves

A question of ownership.

of defining an outline

The limits of a lot.

of forming a figure.

Its chaotic appearance had first
given the illusion it was indeed a
game of chance. But if the
causality had broken under the
simultaneity of the strokes, it
had only been to better multiply
and spread.
The fact is that after a certain
number of attempts, the players
had tried to detect a kind of
A crash of lines tangled up   pattern in the game of their
anyhow   opponent, so as to be able to
                                   counter it in advance.
crumpled a bit too quickly and
thrown in the bin
waiting to go down the stairs
and then what?

The echo of the entrance hall
the smell of the rubbish bins

climbing along the banister
towards the skylight
the corridor
the door?

Too early.
For once
I will have arrived too early
nothing ready

The consequence had tried to
precede the cause. But this
strategy, adopted by both
players, had cancelled each other
out.

like when you put on your best
clothes,
when you change style,
change the way you walk,
when you even change opinions
and all that for a girl you haven't
even met yet.

It had become necessary no
longer only to uncover the logic
of the person opposite but to
evaluate what he had grasped of
your own so as to be able to
discard it. Basically to contradict
yourself, to play against oneself,
the best bit being of course to
willingly fall in one's own traps.
But by wanting to deceive the
idea that you had of how the
other thought you saw yourself
in his own head, the question
had been to know if the two
players hadn't secretly formed
the intention of pulling ahead of
the event by forcing it to cover a
terrible distance in a tunnel with
mirrors. From opponents, they
had become accomplices in a
mutual imposture.

All of it will have been built
around a hollow tooth.
A missing element.
And it is naturally there that I
shall have directed my steps.
Towards the hole in the middle of
the image

the pinhole that will have kept
the image more or less straight on
the wall
the image I shan't have looked at
since I had hung it there
without really knowing why
to give it a place perhaps
to get rid of it most likely
in order to come back to it later
looking at it without seeing it
examining its absence
without the least intention

The theoreticians of game finally
ended up concluding that the
best tactic was undoubtedly to
have none,

and wanting to hide it

and to play each shot as if it was
the first.

anywhere anyhow under the too
dim light

But since one couldn't maintain
the conditions of a big bang per
second, it was agreed that a good
player had realistically to come
under the thin thread of light
barely filtering through the
windows
superimposing the shadows of
the leaves outside with the
shadows from inside
before falling in fine dust
on floors and floors of surfaces
and volumes
arranged at random by a million
isolated actions.

close to the behaviour and degree
of awareness of a rocking chair.
But, by wanting to forget
instantly each attempt, to forget
the beginning of the game and its
whole unfolding so as to avoid
imagining it as a whole and
taking the risk of revealing it to
one's opponent, the players had
almost ended up forgetting that
it had happened.
A question had arisen then rather
naturally. What difference did it
make to have actually played?
The question had generated a
debate spilling beyond the
restricted circle of the amateurs
of the game, each applying
himself reformulating it in his
own way. What difference does it
make having experienced what
you have forgotten? What do you

remember from what you have
forgotten? What is that
forgetting you have an absolute
certainty has happened?

Objects abandoned in the rush
a moment ago.
A few days.

A few volumes had been devoted
to the resolution of that enigma
but the fear that those books
A few years.

might fall into oblivion in their
reader's mind as he made his way
towards their conclusion had

Pompeii of tables and chairs,

pushed the authors to pay
particular attention to the
writing of their postface. The
shortest were, in the general
of glasses scissors screws,

opinion, the most likely to reach
their purpose. By reminding the
reader of the moment when he
hadn't started his reading yet,
pens and books barely formed

they had for function to
determine what difference it
made to have read the book or
not. One of the most used
petrified in full action,

techniques was to encourage the
reader to remember the reason
that had led him to open the
book in the first place and to

suspended in their shared
willingness to be forgotten.
Jumbled assemblage of
miscellaneous matters coming
from who knows where,
from the whole world
to cluster under a too faint light
barely filtering through the
windows
before gathering like puddles,
around my thirsty pupils.
The darkness surrounded from
everywhere
siphoned off through the middle
and only leaving a tiny black hole
a tiny blind spot pinning the
entire picture on the wall of my
retina.

measure then the distance that
separated him now from his
original intention.

To succeed,

the author had
implicitly asked his reader

In order to hold it all together.
To give it a meaning.   to imagine introducing the book
The picture of a man sitting all by   to a third party,
himself in the dark.
Behind his desk
perfectly still   writing down in his head
so as to not be caught unawares
all alone in the dark
like an intruder
that I would almost be scared   a few lines of preface.
shitless just thinking about it
just imagining opening the door
and finding myself like that
face to face with a man
hiding in the shadow   And to end up then,
lifting his head up
haggard   at the moment preceding his
ready to pounce   entrance.

      Between one breath of air

          and the next.

    Between the space you are leaving

        and the space you are joining.

    Between the face you are making

      and the face that is coming.

    Between the voice that speaks

     and the one that

      thinks.

Acknowledgements

I would like to thank Marcelline Delbecq, Gintaras Didžiapetris, Maurizio Gnerre, Yoann Gourmel, Geraldine Longueville, Francesco Pedraglio, Elodie Royer and Bruno Persat.

The Curve of Forgotten Things
Mark Geffriaud

This publication is published
as part of *The Time Machine*,
commissioned by Book Works
and Francesco Pedraglio from
open submission

Published and distributed by
Book Works

Commissioning editor:
Francesco Pedraglio

Edited by Gavin Everall and
Francesco Pedraglio

Preface and postface
translated from the French by
Catherine Petit & Paul Buck

Proofreading by Eileen Daly

Designed by Atelier Dreibholz,
Paulus M. Dreibholz and
Daniel McGhee

Printed by Die Keure, Bruges

ISBN 978 1906012 33 5

Book Works
19 Holywell Row
London EC2A 4JB
www.bookworks.org.uk
tel: +44(0)20 7247 2203

Book Works is funded by Arts
Council England, and this
publication was made
possible with the support of
the French Embassy in the UK